Imagining
What RoBots Can Do
A How to Draw Activity Book

I0080636

ActiviBooks for KiDs

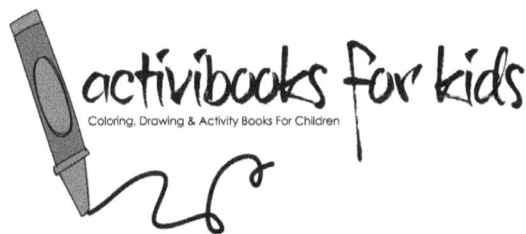

activibooks for kids
Coloring, Drawing & Activity Books For Children

All Rights reserved. No part of this book may be reproduced or used in any way or form or by any means whether electronic or mechanical, this means that you cannot record or photocopy any material ideas or tips that are provided in this book.

Copyright 2016

INSTRUCTIONS FOR DRAWING:

THIS HOW-TO DRAWING BOOK CONSISTS OF IMAGES THAT ARE PLACED ON GRIDS. THERE IS A DRAWING BOX LOCATED AT THE LOWER PART OF THE PAGE AND THAT WILL SERVE AS YOUR PRACTICE SPACE. TO COPY THE IMAGE, DRAW PARTS OF THE IMAGE PER GRID AND PUT THEM ON THE BIGGER GRIDS. SOUNDS DIFFICULT? NOT REALLY. TRY IT FIRST!

IT'S OKAY IF YOU DON'T COPY THE IMAGE PERFECTLY. AFTER ALL, DRAWING IS ABOUT THE EXPRESSION OF YOUR PERCEPTION AS WELL AS YOUR HAND STRENGTH AND CONTROL.

WHEN YOU'VE COPIED THE IMAGE, GO AND AHEAD AND COLOR IT NEXT! WE'RE EXCITED TO SEE WHAT YOU CAN DO!

DRAW THE IMAGE

DRAW
THE
IMAGE

DRAW
THE
IMAGE

DRAW
THE
IMAGE

DRAW
THE
IMAGE

DRAW
THE
IMAGE

DRAW
THE
IMAGE

DRAW
THE
IMAGE

DRAW
THE
IMAGE

DRAW
THE
IMAGE

DRAW
THE
IMAGE

DRAW
THE
IMAGE

DRAW
THE
IMAGE

DRAW
THE
IMAGE

DRAW
THE
IMAGE

DRAW
THE
IMAGE

DRAW
THE
IMAGE

DRAW
THE
IMAGE

DRAW
THE
IMAGE

DRAW
THE
IMAGE

DRAW
THE
IMAGE

DRAW
THE
IMAGE

DRAW
THE
IMAGE

DRAW
THE
IMAGE

DRAW
THE
IMAGE

DRAW
THE
IMAGE

DRAW
THE
IMAGE

DRAW
THE
IMAGE

DRAW
THE
IMAGE

DRAW
THE
IMAGE

DRAW
THE
IMAGE

DRAW
THE
IMAGE

DRAW
THE
IMAGE

DRAW
THE
IMAGE

DRAW
THE
IMAGE

DRAW
THE
IMAGE

DRAW
THE
IMAGE

www.ingramcontent.com/pod-product-compliance
Lightning Source LLC
LaVergne TN
LVHW080249090426
835508LV00042BA/1508